WORD MADE FLESH

JOHN MAIN

Introduction by Laurence Freeman

A Medio Media Book
Continuum • New York

1998
The Continuum Publishing Company
370 Lexington Avenue
New York, NY 10017

Printed in the United States of America

Library of Congress Catalog Card Number 98-73100
ISBN 0-8264-1125-8

Word Made Flesh

Contents

Introduction by Laurence Freeman   vii

Making Progress   1

The Consciousness of Jesus   4

Who is at the Centre?   7

From Idea to Commitment   10

His Time, His Prayer   13

The Universal Christ   16

Making Nothing Happen   19

The Glory of Christ   22

The Unlearning of Prayer   25

The Silence of Love   28

An Ordinary Thing   31

Faith's Transcendence   34

The Gift of Uniqueness   37

I Am as I Am   40

Dropping the Anchor   42

Truth of the Spirit   45

Belief and Faith   48

Contents

All You have to Do is Begin   52

Integrity   55

Purity of Heart   58

Introduction

At the John Main Seminar led by Jean Vanier in London in 1992 the Eucharist on the last day revealed for many of us a most potent hidden sacrament of the Christian tradition. After the gospel Jean Vanier gave the homily and described the 'sacrament' of the washing of the feet. The participants formed small groups of about ten, sat in a circle and silently and reverently in turn washed each other's feet, those whose feet had just been washed placing their hands in silent blessing on the head of the one who had just washed their feet.

This pure theatre opened a new dimension of experience in which the sign that Jesus gave his disciples as their preparation for their last supper together became charged with meaning and presence. It was not the formal gesture of many Holy Thursday liturgies where selected individuals remove one shoe and sock to allow the priest to pour a little water on their foot and dab it with a towel. The footwashing was real. The hands expressed real and tender physical contact and expressed an awareness of love which was more strongly present in the whole group than most knew until they were touched and could touch.

There are of course no new sacraments. But there are new ways of recovering the sense of the sacred which our culture and society so disastrously lacks. Without this spiritual sense we are as actually handicapped as if we lacked any of the five senses to which our concept of reality has so largely been restricted. Indeed if we approach reality only through sight, hearing, touch, taste and smell human consciousness seems to drift away from reality into mere ideas of reality. Sense without spirit becomes senseless.

We are nevertheless a highly sensate culture. Our television screens, stereo systems and advertising posters are obsessed with how we look and feel and smell, what we eat and what music we listen to. Yet the result of all this sensory stimulus is not a heightened consciousness of reality, but the pursuit of 'virtual reality'. We prefer the idealised and controllable images of reality which we can record and replay at will to the real thing. Indeed 'the real thing' has been identified with a fizzy sweet drink which for millions around the world has become a desacralised sacrament of youth, beauty, success and happiness.

> When a man dwells on the pleasures of sense, attraction for them arises in him. From attraction arises desire, the lust of possession, and this leads to passion, to anger. From passion comes confusion of mind, the forgetting of duty.
> From this loss comes the ruin of reason, and the ruin of reason leads man to destruction. But the soul that moves in the world of the senses and yet keeps the senses in harmony, free from attraction and aversion, finds rest in quietness.
> There is no wisdom for a man without harmony, and without harmony there is no contemplation. Without contemplation there cannot be peace, and without peace can there be joy? (Bhagavad Gita 2, 62–66, transl. J. Mascaro, Penguin 1962)

To John Main many Christians are indebted for the rediscovery of a way of prayer, or rather, as he would say, a way into prayer, that frees them from having to approach God from within the confines of virtual reality. The mental imaginative prayer to which most Christians were restricted for many generations frequently denies the one praying the ability to move from image to reality. And as St Gregory of Nyssa said, 'every image of God is an idol'.

Reality is that which we cannot objectify and so it can never be totally rendered into any form whether physical or mental. But the other side of this is that every form, sacred or profane, good or evil, contains a spark of reality and can be a path into reality. St Paul described Jesus as the 'image of the invisible God' and also said that he 'was made sin for us' so that sin in all its forms of illusion might no longer limit our expansion into God.

Much of what religion regards as profane or as an impediment to spiritual progress, such as the body itself, in fact needs to be restored to dignity if progress is to be made. The washing of the feet is a tactile teaching that the 'body is a temple of the Holy Spirit'.

Meditation is a daily teaching through personal experience that reality is whole and cannot be divided. The splintering of reality into sensory or conceptual is reintegrated through meditation. We continue to live in the senses, as the Bhagavad Gita understood, and indeed with a heightened sensory awareness and freedom. But the spiritual sense saves us from thinking that reality can be thought or felt by a detached observer. St Irenaeus taught that God can never be known as an object but only by participation in his own self-knowledge. We know reality only by participating in it. This is why John Main was able to teach meditation with such authority to modern people and why now, ten years since his death, his teaching continues to guide and inspire. Meditation for him was the supremely incarnate way of prayer. It takes the person as a whole into wholeness, into a harmony of body, mind and spirit.

The journey into this fully awakened, fully human state is described once again in this collection of his teachings. It is good to remember they were teachings first delivered to people sitting in readiness for meditation. They should be read with this in mind. And they do indeed make a marvellous preparation for a meditation period, first focusing and then gradually stilling the mind and leading it to the threshold of silence where all words and thoughts are left behind.

Stillness is the way of this journey. As the ego diminishes in the power of silence the meditator expands in what John Main calls the 'freedom from all mental systems and structures'. We become open to the freedom offered us by the gift of being. Our expansion is into the human consciousness of Jesus and our sharing this consciousness, which is one with reality, delivers us from our egotism. It delivers us up to the simplicity of God.

Reality is simple. Virtual reality is infinitely complex. The human mind is a mirror which can reflect itself endlessly and we need in meditation some means as utterly simple as the mantra to lead us through the looking-glass into the real world.

The mantra is a word sacred in one's own tradition which is repeated simply and faithfully throughout the meditation as all other thoughts and images are left behind. The wonder of meditation is that in reality everything which once had the power to limit us, like our senses and our minds, is now charged with the power to be a sacrament of the real.

John Main wanted to lead people to meditation both to discover this for themselves and to teach them that meditation is a serious matter. Not solemn, he would say, as solemnity leads eventually to a lack of reverence. Seriousness on the other hand leads to joy. What is serious about meditation is the discipline it invites us to practise. It is, he says,

> like the practice sessions of an athlete. The iron discipline leads to utter freedom of movement in the art of performance when the discipline itself is transcended.

Understanding this makes the discipline of the mantra, the 'yoke of poverty', understandable as well.

St Bernard spoke of prayer as the process of 'inverbation', the interiorisation and absorption of the Word of God. John Main conveys this universal and profoundly Christian tradition of meditation to us in these pages.

He believed deeply that the meeting of the religions could not be fruitful unless it took place at the spiritual level of this inverbation. The Word of God is not Christian, Buddhist, Hindu or Jewish, Sikh, Zoroastrian, Tantric or Shamanistic. Religions are like the senses of God. Humanity can easily get lost in them and make religion another form of virtual reality. But, like the senses too, religions can sacramentalise God, if we practise them with the sense of the sacred arising from the silence of God within us.

The meeting of religions is the single greatest hope for humanity. If the religions can meet in peace, joy and mutual reverence, every human act of aggression and intolerance is stripped of the justification it claims from its own interpretation of religion. It stands exposed as the naked and ridiculous child-ishness of the isolated ego. The joyful laughter of the Spirit must eventually then bring it to its senses.

This is why it is so important to remind the Christian world of its own gift of meditation. Unless Christians are rooted in this inner experience of their faith their meeting with other religions will lack depth and sincerity. It will almost certainly not be freed from the religious ego's quest for supremacy. But from the inner experience of the reality of Christ the Christian will learn the lesson which Jesus tried and tries to teach his followers:

> After washing their feet and taking his garments again, he sat down. 'Do you understand what I have done for you?' he asked. 'You call me "Master" and "Lord", and rightly so, for that is what I am. Then if I, your Lord and Master, have washed your feet, you also ought to wash one another's feet. I have set you an example: you are to do as I have done for you.' (Jn 13:12–15)

LAURENCE FREEMAN OSB

Making Progress

People often ask me 'what sort of progress can I expect to make in my meditation?' I think it is important for us to understand that our progress is not to be found in anything else but stillness and the fruits of stillness. It is inappropriate to seek for progress in the phenomena of meditation. Don't ask yourself 'am I levitating?' or 'am I seeing visions?'. That has nothing to do with it and in fact if you are seeing visions or levitating it is more likely due to drinking too much soda water than to the Spirit!

Fidelity to the path of meditation allows us to move beyond this kind of materialistic spirituality. Instead we are able to see our progress in the light of a deeper understanding of the meaning of Scripture. Take, for example, these words of St Paul to the Ephesians:

> So he came and proclaimed the good news: peace to you who are far off, and peace to those who are near by; for through him we both alike have access to the Father in the one Spirit. (Eph 2:17)

The message for us here is that Jesus has already achieved all this by opening the highway to the Father for us. We do not have to do anything to bring this about. That is the way it is. We have access to the Father in him and all we have to do is to realise it. Realisation is what meditation is about. The phenomena of 'progress' are utterly unimportant beside the process of realisation which is the opening of our heart, our consciousness, to the great reality that is taking place in our heart. There in our heart the Spirit of Jesus worships and loves the Father and is continuously returning to him in love.

One of the great problems of our contemporary mentality

1

is that we are more concerned with the external phenomena of meditation than with this far more wondrous faith-understanding of it. Thomas a Kempis once wrote that the habit and tonsure contribute little to the essence of the monk. Being a monk, that is, has really nothing to do with externals such as dress or hairstyle. The same is true of meditation. It has nothing essentially to do with externals, such as how you sit or what you look like. It is not essential to sit in the lotus position or to kneel upright. You can meditate in any posture you like, the only basic rule is to have your spine upright and so be alert.

The progress is in the stillness. This is difficult for many to understand today because it so often seems to us we should always be achieving goals. Stillness is not even a goal. It is the absence of effort and the desire to achieve. Learning this is learning how to meditate. Unfortunately so much of modern spirituality thinks in terms of goal-achievement and talks of beginners' and advanced courses. I recently read a programme for a 'School of Spirituality' that went on like this, even saying that you could not progress from one stage to another without requisite credits from earlier courses.

This kind of approach has very little to do with St Paul's message. Because it is all already achieved in Jesus, every one of us has direct access to God in freedom. This freedom from all mental systems and structures is the marvel of the Christian proclamation. It is not something we have to bring about. We are not trying to impose any pattern on reality or to wrench reality in our favour. All we have to do is to be open to the freedom we have been offered. This reality is so overwhelming that when we are open to it there is no room for anything else in our mind or heart. When we have awakened to it in our heart we discover that everything else is contained within it. For this reason meditation is not a state of platonic indifference. It is not a state where we seek to shut out any aspect of reality. Far from it. It is the state of being entirely open to the fullness of reality contained in the love of Jesus as he sweeps us beyond ourselves and beyond himself into the mystery of the limitless love of the Father.

Progress usually implies some way of measurement. But what

we learn is to be faithful. That is the only measure we can apply to meditation. We do this by meditating every morning and evening. It is not enough just to see the vision and to be intoxicated by it. We have to afford it first place in our lives. Meditating each day is nothing but supreme practicality, the way we live each day 'rooted in Christ', in the mystery of reality.

For our heart to be purely open to supreme reality we require the simplicity of a child, to sit still in the presence of God and to remain open at the beginning of each day. Even so, our day can often drift into distraction, meaninglessness, anxiety or illusion. Then the evening meditation again gathers the scattered parts and binds them together in the love of Christ. So do not think of your meditation as the icing on the cake of your day. It is not 'putting a bit of spirituality' into your life. See it rather as informing your whole day with reality: the supreme reality that we now have access to God with freedom.

We are living in the age when the possibilities for the development of human consciousness have been radically transformed by the resurrection of Christ. Every human consciousness has undergone this transformation because in his risen and universal consciousness we have access to the Father, the source and goal of human life and indeed all creation. We live in an age of the infinite mystery realised in Christ and in us. Meditation is simply openness to that reality.

When we start to meditate we have to learn to say, to sound the mantra from the beginning to the end of the meditation. Every meditation is a new experience of this. Starting to sound the mantra silently in our hearts, we then learn to say it continually. When we find we are not saying it or have become distracted we simply return to it gently but with utter fidelity. It is always new. It is always the same.

So when you think of progress think only of progress in stillness. This is the stillness of fidelity. In your physical posture be as still as you can. As your heart fills with wonder at the unfathomable mystery that we are part of, be more deeply still. Progress is only progress in fidelity.

3

The Consciousness of Jesus

The people who seem to misunderstand what meditation is about are often those you would least expect: religious and devout practising Christians. Time and again when I have been talking to such groups they become scandalised at the idea of saying the mantra. It seems to them that the mantra puts God into a strait-jacket and stifles their own spontaneity.

The central reason for this misconception is that so many Christians fail to understand the first principle of Christian prayer. The most important thing to remember is that there is only the prayer of Jesus. This is *the* prayer. His prayer is the torrent of love and power flowing continuously between Jesus and the Father, and that is the Spirit.

This is the first thing for us to try to understand about Christian prayer and of course we cannot understand it. The extraordinary mystery about Christianity is that although we can never understand it we can experience this river of love that pours itself out in the Spirit, and as the Spirit, between Jesus and the Father. We can experience it through the human consciousness of Jesus. This ability to share his consciousness is the Spirit's great gift to us. Indeed it is the meaning of redemption. Our salvation is precisely that in his human consciousness we are delivered out of our own egotism and isolation. The crucifying sense of our separateness and alienation is penetrated and dispelled by the rising within us of the knowledge of our oneness: one with ourselves, with others, with the One who is without a second. Delivered from our egotistical sense of separateness we enter the mystery of God as we travel in that stream of love.

The secret of the Christian revelation to which we are called to open our hearts is that Jesus himself does not ask us to rest in him but to go beyond him to the Father. This is the essence of the Christian mystery – that we transcend self into Jesus and, in him, transcend Jesus into the Father.

The theology of prayer is the theology of the Trinity. When we begin to see it from an experiential standpoint it is simply mind-boggling. The mind cannot hold it together and we must therefore go beyond all concepts of God. We must transcend the language and the insights of the mind because these limit God in our experience. We are called to know God not with our own totally inadequate knowledge but with God's own self-knowledge: the Spirit we receive from Jesus. However perfect or skilled our human mind may be, it is as nothing compared to the wholly ineffable mystery we can enter only by treading the path of simplicity.

It is the simplicity of God, of the divine oneness, that calls us to meditate. It is also our greatest stumbling-block. For how can we with all our complexities know absolute simplicity? The mantra is the way beyond this stumbling-block. It is a sign or symbol of the unity and simplicity of God. In all the classical literature of prayer, in St Teresa, St John of the Cross, Meister Eckhart, for example, we find the common idea that the way to total union and continuous presence is the way of a simple and selfless discipline.

Selflessness is the way of the mantra. It leads us out of the labyrinth of self-consciousness. By its constant repetition it brings us gradually, and with much patience, to the silence where everything is resolved in the utter simplicity of God. In the divine oneness we become one with him. There can be no second, nothing separate. Silence – and meditation is the work of silence – simplifies.

Perhaps the reason too why people so often misunderstand this way of simplicity is because of the patience that is required. We need patiently, day after day, to return to this path of selflessness and silence. It may take people months, even years, just to come to a clear point of beginning, that first degree of unconditional commitment which starts the journey. Yet once you have begun you will find that your daily meditation becomes the great integrating power in your life. It will give depth and perspective to everything you are and everything you do. The simple reason for this is that you are beginning to live from the prime source of integrity, of wholeness, the God who alone is holy. You begin to live out of the power of this love of God that is one, that is the creative origin of all that is and that unifies all with itself.

This power in all its immensity and simplicity is present in our hearts in the consciousness of Jesus. The integrating power of meditation affects every part of our life. Every part is reconciled to the whole. All our life is aligned on Christ, and his presence makes itself felt in every part. The way to this is the way of humility and self-knowledge, of simplicity and silence, the way of the mantra.

Be humble always and gentle, and patient too. Be forbearing with one another and charitable. Spare no effort to make fast with bonds of peace the unity which the Spirit gives. (Eph 4:3)

Who is at the Centre?

I was giving a talk recently to a group of people who were all sincerely interested in meditation. But quite a few were wondering 'was this really for them' and one person asked if I could put very simply, and in a couple of sentences, what is the 'essence of meditation'. I took some time to think this out, because it was a sincere and important question and because it should be possible to put anything important in a few words, although those words may vary according to who you are speaking to and when.

It seemed to me then that the best way to put it was that meditation, in essence, is learning to stand back and to allow God to come to the forefront of life. So often in our experience we find that we have put ourselves at the centre of the world. Sometimes this is a rude awakening. We realise that we are seeing reality revolve around us. We think and react quite automatically to situations and to people primarily in terms of how they affect ourselves. This self-centred vision is all right as far as it goes. It has a certain practical necessity to it. But the vital question is, do we know how far it goes? If we actually imagine and take for granted that we are the centre of the world we will never be able to see any situation or any person, or even ourselves, as they really are. Because, of course, the truth is we are not at the centre of the world. God is the centre.

Meditation is the step away from self-centredness to God-centredness. In taking that step we find our own place in the world, where we should be and where we truly are. All our relationships are consequently put into a right order: our relationships with one another, with the environment and all creation, our relationship with God. Then we discover, and it is vital for our health that each of us does discover it, that we

7

do have an essential place in God's plan. It is perhaps the most important thing for people in our society today to discover the dignity of responding to the unique gift of our own creation.

How can we set about doing this? Meditation is the discipline of doing it. Its discipline is that we learn to stand back and to focus our attention, our whole being, on God. We have to begin somewhere. We have to begin with ourselves and by learning to be silent with ourselves. This means simply learning to be, to be ourselves, rather than defining ourselves by what we do or what we think. As an art and a practice, meditation brings us towards this state of simple being through the still, silent repetition of the mantra.

The purpose of saying the mantra is that it becomes the focus of your attention. We are not thinking of anything nor are we pursuing any insights that may come to us as we say the mantra. Let them all fall away as you come to an ever deeper silence in which the only sound in your mind is the mantra. The mantra itself will teach you the patience needed to say it. It will also teach you the humility needed. In meditating we are not seeking to possess God or to arrive at a profound insight about God. We are seeking simply to accept the gift of our own creation as fully as we presently can and to respond to it as generously as we can. To do this we learn to be still, to be silent and to be truly humble.

In commonday language, the essence of meditation is to leave the ego behind. We are not trying to see with the ego what is happening. Ego-vision is limited by its own self-centredness. The eye with which we see without limit is the eye that cannot see itself. The paradox of meditation is that once we give up trying to see and to possess, then we see all and all things are ours.

In beginning to meditate, as in persevering, the essential understanding we need to have grasped is the simplicity of it. The simplicity is just this: that every morning and each evening you give yourself the opportunity to be. You are simple because you are not asking yourself 'what is happening to me now?' You are not analysing yourself, nor are you evaluating yourself. You are not saying 'am I enjoying this?' or 'am I getting anything out of this?' During this time of being put the self-reflective ego entirely aside.

You will have to begin in faith. There is no way you can evaluate what is happening when you begin. Later, you will not bother to try to evaluate it. Because meditation is a way of faith you cannot just have a curious stab at it, saying your mantra for three minutes, then stopping to see how you're doing. You learn to say your word from the beginning to the end, every day. This is to be done without the strain of force. The art is setting the word free in your heart, not trying to dominate or control with the word. Only say the word and be.

Where does this connect with Christian faith? In Christian terms, we know that God has sent his Spirit to dwell in us through the human consciousness of Jesus. His being is within us. Meditating is simply being open to his being.

> For the same God who said, 'Out of darkness let light shine', has caused his light to shine within us, to give us the light of revelation – the revelation of the glory of God in the face of Jesus Christ. (2 Cor 4:6)

This light and glory are to be found in our hearts if only we will learn to be still, to be silent and to be humble. That is the exact purpose of the mantra.

From Idea to Commitment

One of the difficulties in talking to people for the first time about meditation is that so many are looking for its intellectual content. The problem is that there is no intellectual content. Silence takes us beyond all that because the truth we are open to in meditation is itself beyond the intellect.

Jesus spoke of this truth not as an intellectual formula but as a call to union.

> May they all be one: as thou, Father, art in me, and I in thee, so also may they be in us. (Jn 17:21)

This is not easy or possible to encapsulate in an intellectual way. St Thomas Aquinas called the union of Jesus with the Father a 'substantial union'. His idea has value but it is limited by the language, the meaning of the words themselves, the understanding of the listener. Today we would probably say that the union of Jesus with the Father is a union in essence and that the essence of the Godhead is found in the union. It is the same kind of union – from essence to essence – that characterises the presence of the Spirit of Jesus in our spirit. But we seek to be open to this truth in meditation not at the level of intellectual awareness but at the level of spiritual knowledge. Here it is not ideas that move us but the movement of love itself, the self-communicating love of the Spirit expressing itself perfectly and without distortion in silence.

But at times other than meditation it is difficult to disentangle ourselves from the idea that we can encapsulate God in our own little intellectual formulas. This is why we need to nourish our minds frequently with the word of Scripture because here we learn of the limitations. And in accepting them we are free of them.

We are no better than pots of earthenware to contain this treasure, and this proves that such transcendent power does not come from us, but is God's alone. . . Wherever we go we carry death with us in our body, the death that Jesus died, that in this body also life may reveal itself, the life that Jesus lives. (2 Cor 4:7, 10)

From intellectual questioning we move through silence to commitment. We are committed to the truth that death and the life of Jesus are to be found in each of us. That death is death to all limitation, including the limitation that any intellectual formula and any thought we could have imposes on God.

The extraordinary thing about the Christian proclamation is that every one of us is invited to the utter liberty of spirit in the life that follows this death. We leave behind all created limitations in the human consciousness of Jesus which has transcended them all.

The purpose of meditation is nothing less than this. But make no mistake about the commitment to discipline that it entails, the discipline of putting aside every limitation whether in the form of words, ideas, images, insights or symbols.

Meditation is like the practice sessions of an athlete. The iron discipline leads to utter freedom of movement in the art of the performance when the discipline itself is transcended. The difficulty of not understanding this is that it leads people to say things like 'I meditate a bit. In my own way. I say a word occasionally. When it feels right. What's all this fuss about utter commitment?' To this mentality, indeed, saying the mantra for the full period of the meditation seems like a substantial union with the essence of utter rigidity and self-restriction. It seems, they might say, like putting the Holy Spirit in a strait-jacket. But, as anyone who has practised this discipline knows, you cannot even begin to try to put the Holy Spirit in a strait-jacket. Although you can begin to say the mantra, from beginning to end, you say it until you can say it no longer and then, if there is a strait-jacket around, it is the Holy Spirit who puts you in it: the strait-jacket of unavoidable liberty. In the utter silence there is only God, there is only oneness and it is the oneness that is 'all in all'.

11

We must be always careful that thought of the goal does not deflect us from understanding the means necessary to reach it. The means are as utterly simple as to meditate every morning and evening and during the meditation to say our word from beginning to end. Thus we turn from all day-dreaming, from all holy floating and self-dialogue. Thus we gradually submit ourselves to the yoke of poverty. It is the poverty of the 'one little word' which requires the faith of commitment. There are no half-measures possible. You cannot meditate a bit. You either say your word or you do not.

I suppose it is the completeness of the commitment that frightens us. But commit yourself but once and you will know from your own experience the love that casts out all fear. It takes many people years to come to that moment of commitment. Yet whether it takes years, months, weeks, or days, is of no importance. All that is important is that each of us, as best we can in these earthen vessels, is as open as we can be to the essential truth of union. We are invited to be in the 'all in all'. As far as we can see with our limited insight, the way to the necessary commitment for this union is the way of poverty, silence and humility – the way of the mantra.

His Time, His Prayer

In beginning to meditate we have usually to face the question, 'What should my expectations be?' What should we expect to happen? To approach meditation like this, however, is rather like approaching breathing and asking 'what will happen as the result of my breathing?' What happens when you breathe is that you live. Your vitality is assured with every breath. Meditation is very like that. Nothing dramatic happens except that your spirit breathes. You also come to a vitality of spirit very similar to the vitality that your body enjoys as a result of your breathing.

But it is very difficult for us to approach meditation without expecting some kind of payoff for what we are putting into it. As Westerners we think in terms of the production line and we judge in terms of profit and loss. When we are told to meditate for half an hour morning and evening it seems like a big investment of time and effort and we want to know what the return is going to be. Meditation cannot be reduced to a commodity like this and the spiritual tradition is not a supermarket to shop in or a stock market to gamble on.

Because we think in these terms, however, there can be a real danger that meditation is presented in terms of return and payoff. Most of the books on meditation in the bookshops offer a whole list of returns from lowering your blood pressure to better exam results and levitation. But whether any of these results, some reasonable, some false, occur at all is not of the slightest importance. The only important thing is that your spirit lives, that it lives wholly and that it realises its union with God and with all.

So, a quality you require for meditation is simplicity. You have to learn just to sit down and to do it.

They brought babies for him to touch; but when the disciples saw them they scolded them for it. But Jesus called for the children and said 'Let the little ones come to me; do not try to stop them; for the kingdom of God belongs to such as these. I tell you whoever does not accept the kingdom of God like a child will never enter it.' (Luke 18: 15–17)

The 'kingdom of God' is a biblical phrase for God's power. It is the power of love established in our hearts. The marvel about the proclamation of the New Testament is that each of us is called to realise that this power is really and presently in our heart. To realise it is to enter it like a mighty torrent.

To come to that realisation we need simplicity. We must become like children so that we can say 'Abba, Father' in the consciousness that we are ourselves and God is God. Perhaps the most important demand on people of our time is to come to the understanding that we are good and have a capacity for goodness. It is a goodness that cannot be measured, only known in relation to the infinity of God and the boundless Spirit that lives in our heart.

Once our spirit is opened to the Spirit of God, division is over. We do not have to play games any more. We can act consistently from our deepest integrity. Nothing can divide our heart once we are open to the Spirit. We have only to learn generosity of heart to be wholly at the disposition of God in the utter openness of love, without demands or expectations of reward.

My advice is to see your times of meditation not as times that are at your disposition at all. See your meditation, your prayer, not as your own but as the prayer of Jesus. As long as we are self-importantly thinking of our meditation, or our prayer, we have not fully started this pilgrimage. The time is his, the prayer is his. The miracle is that his prayer is ours, and the miracle is worked by simplicity bringing us to that total and unshakeable confidence in the Father which the Gospel describes as hope. We approach meditation with hope rather than desire: without hesitation and with a childlike sense of being available to God.

We learn therefore to say the mantra with this same simplicity. We are not analysing it, or its effect, in a calculating way. We say it with a wholly sincere, self-emptying love. Yet by virtue of this self-emptying we are filled with the power of God and with the knowledge that we are one with God because we are lovable and loved. The only requirement is total selflessness expressed in the total abandoning of all our own thoughts, imagination, insights and, above all, our own prayers. This is our openness to the prayer of Jesus in our heart.

The ancient writers called meditation the practice of purity of heart. We have to purify, which means to clarify, our consciousness so that we can see with perfect clarity of vision. What we see is what is there. We see ourselves. We see creation. We see God. In his light we see light.

The revelation of all this is his. We learn from the faithfulness of our daily meditation how to wait on God and to attend to God in the deepening patience of true presence and mindfulness. In a growing fidelity and clarity of consciousness I urge you to put aside all the irrelevant kinds of speculation: am I enjoying this, am I getting anything out of this, am I becoming wiser or holier?

We know that there is a pilgrimage to make. It is the journey away from self and into the mystery of God. It is an amazing grace that each of us can and does know this, or at least suspect it. To know it is really to know everything because then we have only to begin and to continue. To be on the pilgrimage is everything.

We must learn to become simple, one, whole. We must learn to become peace, so that we become ourselves. In meditation we learn to be and in learning this we learn with unshakeable certainty that God is. When you meditate, sit upright, close your eyes and say your word, without speculation, without self-consciousness, without haste, simply like a child, until the end of the meditation.

The Universal Christ

In the experience of meditation we discover a growing awareness of unity. The mantra, as I have said before, is like a
harmonic that sounds within and brings us into a harmonious
unity with the whole of creation, within and without. It is like
– I am talking poetically – the harmonic of God bringing us
into harmony and union with God himself. This experience of
unity inspired St Paul's vision of the cosmic Christ filling the
whole universe and leaving no part of it untouched by his
redemptive love.

> In him everything in heaven and on earth was created, not
> only things visible but also the invisible orders . . . the whole
> universe has been created through him and for him. (Col
> 1:16)

Through the experience of meditation we come to understand that each of us, meaning every living human being, is in
a creative relationship with God through Christ. Meditation
has such great importance because as each of us comes closer
to Christ the whole fabric of human consciousness is knit more
closely together. When we come to see this as individuals we
also come to realise that the development of our own personal
consciousness and the deepening of our own spiritual journey
is not just a personal matter. It partakes of a responsibility for
the whole human race. Meditation teaches us something more:
that the more deeply we enter into this mystery of unity the
more truly human and humane we become. By deepening our
commitment to our own human journey each of us is also
deepening our commitment to the whole of humanity, in particular of course to that part of humanity that we encounter in
our daily round.

This is to say our commitment is to the universal Christ. Even more, if that is possible, it is a commitment to the whole creation. This means a committed concern and compassion for the beauty of nature, and of the human spirit expressed in art, a respect for the environment and all it encapsulates in terms of value and beauty. Every part of life is deepened as we enter the mystery of the universal Christ.

The longer we meditate the more we see that this vision is one of infinite depth and boundless proportion. But we should never allow the wonder of this vision to blind us to the need for daily fidelity and daily humility.

I was talking to someone today who asked if there wasn't a real danger that, if you were too open to this cosmic vision of St Paul, you would become a really arrogant person, who thought you knew it all, with all the answers and a cold detachment from the needs or sufferings of others. The answer to that, I think, is that anyone who has tried to say their mantra with daily and deepening fidelity has every reason to grow in humility.

Meditation in this sense is a total ascesis. And ascesis is the antidote for arrogance. It is a path to ground you more and more in the strength, the 'virtue', of Christ. You thus become aware that strength comes from beyond yourself, is greater than you and contains you. Yet it is your strength. This is the mystery of the experience of prayer, that the power released in your heart is your power because it is the power of God. Learning to say the mantra is learning to receive everything from God but to receive it fully, not passively or half-heartedly. We respond in meditation with our whole being to the gift of our whole creation. Prayer realises this inherent potential for expanding in spirit, in union.

As always, we return to the mantra because to see the vision we must become still. To come into contact with God's Spirit in your heart you must come into contact with your own spirit in the simplicity of utter stillness. That is why we must go beyond all analysis, all division and observation and move into unity. And then we move from unity to union.

I don't think we need to be bothered about becoming arrogant. We need only be bothered about fidelity – fidelity to the daily return to meditation and during meditation to the mantra. However often we are taught this we only realise it in the practice of meditation. It was the one teaching my own teacher gave me. And now, thirty years down the road, I realise it is teaching of the most extraordinary wisdom.

Making Nothing Happen

The questions people most frequently raise when they first encounter meditation express the deep puzzlement of our culture with this ancient spiritual tradition. They ask 'what are we trying to do . . . what's supposed to happen?'

One of the most difficult things for Westerners to understand is that meditation is not about trying to make anything happen. But all of us are so tied into the mentality of techniques and production that we inevitably first think that we are trying to engineer an event, a happening. According to our imagination or predispositions, we may have different ideas of what should happen. For some it is visions, voices or flashes of light. For others, deep insights and understanding. For others again, better control over their daily lives and problems. The first thing to understand, however, is that meditation is nothing to do with making anything happen. The basic aim of meditation is indeed quite the contrary, simply to learn to become fully aware of what is. The great challenge of meditation is to learn directly from the reality that sustains us.

The first step towards this – and we are all invited to take it – is to come into contact with our own spirit. Perhaps the greatest tragedy of all is that we should complete our life without ever having made full contact with our own spirit. This contact means discovering the harmony of our being, our potential for growth, our wholeness – everything that the New Testament, and Jesus himself, called 'fullness of life'.

So often we live our life at five per cent of our full potential. But of course there is no measure to our potential; the Christian tradition tells us it is infinite. If only we will turn from self to other our expansion of spirit becomes boundless. It is all-turning: what the New Testament calls conversion. We are invited to unlock the shackles of limitation, to be freed from being prisoners within our self-limiting egos. Conversion is just this liberation and expansion arising when we turn from ourselves to the infinite God. It is also learning to love God, just as in turning to God we learn to love one another. In loving we are enriched beyond measure. We learn to live out of the infinite riches of God.

Biblically, conversion had two aspects. There was the ritual, exterior conversion typified, for example, by putting on ashes and rending garments. But the constant theme of the prophets and throughout biblical history is that this external conversion is of no use unless it is inspired and springs from an inner conversion of heart. The prophet Joel cries, therefore, 'this people honours me with their lips but their heart is far from me.'

Meditation is about deep conversion of heart. Religion is meaningless if it is confined to external and ritual acts of worship. Liturgy and ritual only have meaning when they are inspired by conversion of heart. This is what we are turning to as we learn to be still. In stillness an awareness matures that God has revealed himself to humanity in Jesus and that Jesus reveals himself to us, in our heart, by his Spirit which he has sent to dwell within us. Our life, no less than liturgy, finds meaning when we are as fully open as we can be to this Spirit.

Looked at from the outside, meditation can be thought of as a static condition, one in which you had closed down the doors of perception. But from actual experience meditation is known to be far from a static state and is far better understood as a dynamic awakening to the fullness of your own potential for development. The expansion of our spirit in the love of Jesus is this fullness. Simplicity, childlike trust and wonder are the ways to realise it. We are not looking for anything to happen, for any insights or wisdom. We are not analysing any superficial or external phenomena. All this is trivia compared with the knowledge of the Spirit dwelling within us that arises when we turn our minds aside from what is temporal and passing and instead open our hearts to what is enduring: God and God's love for each of us. This is how we discover our love for all our brothers and sisters, knowing that we are loved.

Don't neglect the discipline of stillness of body when you meditate. Remind yourself of it periodically in case you have started to get a little indulgent with your fidgeting. In saying the mantra you can breathe it in in one breath and breathe out silently. Then, in saying your mantra, it is as if you are accepting God's Spirit, which is your life. You breathe it in. And breathing out in silence is like returning your life to God in absolute faith and with absolute love, ready to receive it from him again should he give it back to you. Our breath shows how meditation is firmly anchored in the essential axis of the Christian revelation: death and resurrection. We die to everything that is passing away. Life is into the infinite God.

It is nothing less than essential to meditate every day. Meditation is to the spirit what food and air are to the body. We must come to peacefulness, serenity and our capacity for true vision if we are to live in the light of God. Again and again the New Testament tells us that the light shines in our hearts. So we need only be open to it in humility and love. That is why we should try to the best of our ability to find a time and a place each morning and evening to turn aside from what is passing away and to be open to what is eternal. The most extraordinary mystery of our life is found in this conversion: that what is eternal is love, is God and dwells in our heart.

> What we have seen and heard we declare to you, so that you and we together may share in a common life, that life which we share with the Father and with his Son Jesus Christ. And we write this in order that the joy of us all may be complete. (1 Jn 1:3–4)

This is the Christian vision. It is the Christian message that we are invited to share in the light of God and in God's very being.

The Glory of Christ

I would like to turn here to the idea of the glory of God in the New Testament. But I am well aware of how easily we can become intoxicated on ideas and words. How important it is to remember the simplicity of meditation and the need for daily fidelity. Just how easily words can miss the mark was brought home to me recently when I was giving a series of talks on meditation. Somebody told me how he came in to the last talk and sat down beside a man who had been fervently attending the whole series and had sat very attentively in the front seat. The newcomer asked him if he had found the talks useful. 'Oh yes,' the man replied, 'it's been fantastic. This fellow is very interesting. You see he's got this Arabic word. Apparently you just sit relaxed and close your eyes and say this word – and you get the most wonderful ideas coming into your head. It's great and, you know, it really works!'

The glory of God is something different from all the wonderful ideas that float through our minds in our pious day-dreaming sessions. It is the experience of the power of Christ that arises in faith. To be a Christian means to enjoy this faith and this in turn means being open to his power. Faith is essentially our sustained openness to his power. For the key teachers of faith in the letters of the New Testament, Paul, Peter and John, the power of Jesus is his 'glory' and this is seen as nothing less than the light that shines through the whole universe. Most extraordinarily it also shines in our hearts. It is pure consciousness. It is absolute love. It is of God.

Meditation is the way to the most profound openness to this power, light and glory of which we are capable in this life. But anyone interested in meditation should understand from the outset that once this power begins to have its way and this light begins to shine undimmed in our hearts, we are transformed. In becoming ourselves we are never the same again. Life is itself transfigured because we begin to live from the vitalising power of the supreme glory of Jesus which is his love.

We could say that the glory of Jesus is the result of his pure receptivity and total openness to the love of the Father. It is our destiny to be receptive to his love and so to return with him to the Father. The dimensions of this destiny escape our minds. And words are only words. Yet the words have the limited value of calling us to be open to all this, not as words or concepts but as reality. Such radical and simple openness requires discipline and fidelity: the kind of faithful discipline we practise each day in returning to our word.

In faithfulness we learn faith. We learn to go into the dark, that expanse of consciousness which lies beyond the little island lit by our ego. We learn to go into the silence where there is no sound and to go ever deeper into the silence of the mystery of God. In meditation we learn the courage to launch out into the deep. From those depths come the power and the glory of the resurrection. Here is the new life given back to Jesus by his Father that places him in the divine aura of glory for ever. His new life, glory and power – all words struggling to express the dimensions of love – are ours. The mystery that renews our hold on life once we enter it is that we, very ordinary people, are to be transformed in Christ. We have only to be mindful and so to realise from our own experience everything that has been achieved for us by Jesus.

The Jesus of the New Testament is the archetypal man of faith. It is through his faithfulness that the Father raises him to glory. It is our way of faith that leads us to share in the glory of Christ that is enshrined in the heart of each of us. Gradually we are transformed by this glory, if we can give it full sway and so allow it to become the supreme power in our life. It is this power of Jesus' glory that empowers us to be one with him in his suffering and death and also in his resurrection to new and limitless life. Christian prayer is this experience. An utterly transforming liberty of spirit is released within our hearts and in our freedom we are able to embrace our destiny which is to share fully in the glory and the power of the love of Jesus.

This language is of course traditional. Putting it in other terms we could say that meditation is so important because it is the pure consciousness of Jesus that burns away our ego. His glory is the power of a fully realised humanity, and to become engaged in a relationship with this humanity enables us to act beyond the confines of our self-perceived and often self-defined limitations. Glory is what burns away sinfulness – 'as if there were no such cold thing'. The Christian way is to be centred in Christ rather than in the illusions of our egotistical self-imprisonment. We don't have to concentrate on our illusions or sinful tendencies but simply – and this does not mean easily – to allow the glory of Christ to burn them away, revealing them all as the sham they are. Glory entirely dissipates whatever is inglorious.

We need to remember today that this is what Christian prayer is about. Not the self-rejection of mock humility. Not egocentric dependence on or fear of a parental god. Not psychological games with our own minds. But transformation in glory. It is about living in harmony with the mystery of God in the depth of being. And because this is to be rooted in reality it is known by being rooted in joy and in love. Prayer is utterly realistic and the indispensable component of healthy realism. The only reality is God who is love, and the power and glory of this love are to be found within our heart – if we seek it. And if we seek it we find it. This seeking is the pilgrimage.

> Praise be to the God and Father of our Lord Jesus Christ, who has bestowed on us in Christ every spiritual blessing in the heavenly realms. In Christ he chose us before the world was founded, to be dedicated, to be without blemish in his sight, to be full of love; and he destined us – such was his will and pleasure – to be accepted as his children through Jesus Christ, in order that the glory of his gracious gift, so graciously bestowed on us in his Beloved, might redound to his praise. . . Therein lies the richness of God's free grace lavished upon us, imparting full wisdom and insight. (Eph 1:3–8)

The Unlearning of Prayer

So much depends upon being clear from the start what are the essential points to understand about meditation. Even though meditation itself is not about thinking, the wrong thinking can delay our start or disturb the smoothness of the journey. The greatest challenge in this regard is probably the sheer simplicity of meditation. We are not used to thinking of anything really simple as really worthwhile. Complexity seems to be worthier of respect, according to the way we are brought up. The more complex a science is, the greater the intelligence required to unravel it and therefore the greater respect we have for it. But as St John of the Cross says, learning to pray means unlearning everything else. It is the unlearning that poses the difficulty for us and it is here we are most likely to get our ideas wrong.

Unlearning can sound like a crude or naive kind of anti-intellectualism. But consider the truth we are dealing with at this level of faith. It is not a mechanical, chemical, biological or scientific truth.

> Continually, while still alive, we are being surrendered into the hands of death, for Jesus' sake, so that the life of Jesus also may be revealed in this mortal body of ours. (2 Cor 4:11)

It is the conviction of the early Church – their conviction being an experience of the truth – that the life of Jesus is being progressively and more profoundly revealed within and through each one of us. At one level we all know this essential theology. How do we respond to this?

Collectively our response is the Christian tradition. It has many strands, themes and many great voices. Concerning prayer, the tradition teaches us that Christianity is not basically a theology or an ideology. It does not have its fullest life in the mind. It is, most truly, a personal and total openness to the person of Jesus. In that openness we are taken by him to the Father. Christianity is the religion of transcendence which sees us transcending our own limited life and entering the limitless life of God.

We teach meditation in a tradition of prayer that unites John Cassian and the Desert Fathers to *The Cloud of Unknowing* in the fourteenth century and, for example, Abbot John Chapman in the twentieth century. It teaches that the essential way to respond to the basic Christian truth is to be fully open to the reality of the life of Jesus within us, deeper than thoughts or words can reach. It teaches us that the way to this depth is a spiritual discipleship. We must learn to be disciplined. The essential discipline is nothing less than leaving self behind. This means leaving behind those limitations with which we so often identify ourselves and learning to be open to the limitless being of God. This teaching enshrines an astonishing Christian doctrine.

> Indeed, it is for your sake that all things are ordered, so that, as the abounding grace of God is shared by more and more, the greater may be the cause of thanksgiving that ascends to the glory of God. (2 Cor 4:15)

Quite specifically in this tradition there is the teaching of the prayer of one word: to sit in stillness and silence and interiorly repeat your word in faith. As the inheritors of this tradition at the end of the twentieth century we can see how precious and valuable it has been for us whose prayer had become so mentally compartmentalised and arid. Meditation is our response to the essential truth of the gospel. But it is not thinking about God, about theology or about religion. It is not about thinking. It is being with God.

When you begin you have to take this truth on faith. You can take it on the faith of godly men and women throughout the ages who have confronted the basic theology that Jesus lives and that he lives in our hearts. They have sought to make the truth of it the main thrust of their lives. They have taught us to concentrate the whole of our being in the recital of what *The Cloud of Unknowing* calls the 'one little word'.

Reciting the word will teach you many things. Humility. Poverty. Fidelity. Hope. In surrendering all the richness of words and all ideas you can be open to the supreme reality, the infinity of God which cannot be captured in any concept but can be encountered in your own heart. Learning to pray is not a matter of listening to talks or reading books on prayer. It can only happen if you pray and all we can do in prayer is to dispose ourselves.

The gift is given, the Spirit is in the heart. All prayer is the pure gift of God given to us with infinite generosity. God can only give in an infinitely generous way. Meditating is a small token of our reciprocal generosity in our openness to his gift. I recommend you, therefore, to see those two daily periods of meditation as God's times not your own. Approaching it in this way, rather than thinking of it as a way to get something out of it, will help you to build up your fidelity.

Only two things are necessary: to be faithful every day to your meditation each morning and evening; and to be faithful during your meditation to the recitation of the word from the beginning to the end. That faithfulness opens your heart to the infinite generosity of God.

But to this very day, every time the Law of Moses is read, a veil lies over the minds of the hearers. However, as Scripture says of Moses, 'whenever he turns to the Lord the veil is removed'. Now the Lord of whom this passage speaks is the Spirit; and where the Spirit of the Lord is, there is liberty. And because for us there is no veil over the face, we all reflect as in a mirror the splendour of the Lord; and thus we are transfigured into his likeness, from splendour to splendour; such is the influence of the Lord who is Spirit. (2 Cor 3:15–18)

The Silence of Love

St Augustine's memorable sentence speaks freshly to every generation of Christians: 'My heart is restless until it rests in Thee'. It is the universal and perennial human search to find that rest and to realise that to find rest is to face the challenge of coming down to reality. We need to find the really solid base out of which we live. So much of life is passing away. The business of living is like sand running through an hour-glass. But as we see the sand falling through we all know that this cannot be all there is. We know that there must be something more solid and enduring.

We know something else too. We know that we are not meant only to find and look at this rocklike base of reality but we are summoned to live fully from that base. This is the experience of liberty as described in the New Testament. Having been rooted and grounded in the solid rock that is Christ, we then live 'in Christ' so that our lives and their horizon begin to expand. This is the Christian experience. Our invitation is to live not just our own isolated lives, but to live out of the infinity of God – or, rather, *into* the infinity of God. The experience of meditation is about this rooted living in Christ. We find ourselves within his mystery and we lose ourselves within it.

Out of, into. Losing, finding. This is the trouble in talking about meditation. Whatever language we use begins to falsify some aspect of the experience as soon as we begin to use it. If I speak of 'losing our life' I cannot explain to you how fully and how profoundly our life is given to us. The idea of loss misses our deep awareness of life as an absolute gift, something that is not falling through the hour-glass but is expanding into eternity.

Language is so weak in explaining the fullness of the mystery. That is why the absolute silence of meditation is so supremely important. We do not try to think of God, talk to God or imagine God. We stay in that awesome silence open to the eternal silence of God. We discover in meditation, through practice and taught daily by experience, that this is the natural ambience for all of us. We are created for this and our being flourishes and expands in that eternal silence.

'Silence', as a word, however, already falsifies the experience and perhaps deters many people, because it suggests some negative experience, the deprivation of sound or language. People fear that the silence of meditation is regressive. But experience and tradition teach us that the silence of prayer is not the pre-linguistic but the post-linguistic state in which language has completed its task of pointing us through and beyond itself and the whole realm of mental consciousness. The eternal silence is not deprived of anything nor does it deprive us of anything. It is the silence of love, of unqualified and unconditional acceptance. We rest there with our Father who invites us to be there, who loves us to be there and who has created us to be there.

The only language in which we can adequately speak of meditation is a language of opposites and balanced contradictions. We have to speak negatively in order to try to understand all the positive aspects of God's simple and mysterious unity.

> If you love me you will obey my commands; and I will ask the Father, and he will give you another to be your Advocate, who will be with you for ever – the Spirit of truth. The world cannot receive him, because the world neither sees nor knows him; but you know him, because he dwells with you and is in you. I will not leave you bereft; I am coming back to you. In a little while the world will see me no longer, but you will see me; because I live, you too will live; then you will know that I am in my Father, and you in me and I in you. (Jn 14:15–20)

The greatest of all paradoxes is contained in these words which are among the most extraordinary ever composed. In them we see the mystery of personal being within universal unity. This is what Christianity teaches. Its simple rendering of this truth is that the Father loves us. But because language fails us this simple truth can be misunderstood, dismissed, scorned.

Yet the Christian life is the ever deeper exploration of the truth that God loves us and that Jesus dwells in our hearts, in the deep centre of our being. Even more astonishing is to know that we dwell in his heart, 'in him'. The mind cannot comprehend this. Only the heart can know it because it is the knowledge that arises only in love.

We know ourselves loved and so we love. Meditation is concerned with completing this cycle of love. By our openness to the Spirit who dwells in our hearts, and who in silence is loving to all, we begin the journey of faith. We end in faith because there is always a new beginning to the eternal dance of being-in-love.

Faith and love engender hope. Christian hope is the supreme confidence in the truthfulness of Jesus and in the reality of his love. This confidence enables us to say the mantra. We let go of everything that we want, everything we know and by which we know that we are. We let it go in the abandon of poverty; and we are then free to launch out into the depths of the mystery that is love, faith and supreme confidence.

Because I live, you too will live; then you will know that I am in my Father, and you in me and I in you.

This is why we leave all words behind and learn to be still: still in body, still in mind, still in spirit. Rooted in our word, rooted in Jesus and rooted in love – for one another and in him.

An Ordinary Thing

When you begin to meditate it may seem strange because the experience seems unfamiliar. In fact it is no stranger than being ourselves, but often we have become strangers to ourselves. As the experience becomes more integrated we soon realise what a very ordinary thing meditation is.

Unfortunately in our complex and self-conscious society we think of meditation as something extraordinary. Yet it is something for which each of us was created: to be simple, to be one and to flourish in the state of absolute oneness and peace. Meditation is that most ordinary part of our daily life when we are most our self. In stillness we are simply ourselves, neither remembering our past selves nor straining to become any other self. In stillness we are more and more deeply rooted in God, the creator-source and the supreme self, the 'great I am'. At these times of supreme ordinariness we are living out of the depths of that eternal selfhood not the shallows of our ego-identities. The power of our being is ours in God.

One of the mysteries we have lost contact with in Christianity in recent times is the fullness of this power bestowed as a gift on each of us.

> I thank God for all the enrichment that has come to you in Christ. You possess full knowledge and you can give full expression to it, because in you the evidence for the truth of Christ has found confirmation. . . It is God himself who called you to share in the life of his Son Jesus Christ our Lord; and God keeps faith. (1 Cor 1:5–6, 9)

Each Christian must once again understand that this is his and her vocation. Each of us is called to share in the fullness of the life of Jesus. Christianity is not primarily concerned with

31

knowledge of God or knowledge about God. It is concerned with coming to knowledge in God. This sums up the whole purpose of meditation. Its aim is not to be thinking of ourselves or to be thinking about God. That is the last thing we should be doing in meditation. Meditation is rather the way, the pilgrimage, along which we come to full knowledge in God. We cannot understand this. We can only know it in simplicity, in silence and in stillness.

Meditation is so simple that this is part of the difficulty. People in our sort of complex society are trained only to give their faith to what is complex. That is why it is probably helpful for people to go along to meditation groups several weeks in a row and to share again and again the simplicity involved in meditation. They can learn the essentials of simplicity and hear some of the ordinary things that make it easier to be simple – taking off your shoes, perhaps, not wearing tight clothing, sitting upright.

Meditation is a discipline of simplicity. Our world needs to learn it urgently. It is a discipline whereby you direct all your powers of consciousness to God. Instead of being at the mercy of your mind with its myriad thoughts and imaginations you bring your mind, your consciousness, to silence. In that silence you quite naturally become open to God and God's power. It is an utterly benevolent power which we can only describe with the word 'love'.

Gradually, as we progress in meditation, in fidelity, simplicity and silence, we come to harmonise with that power of love. As we do so, we learn that it is the universal human call to be so wholly at one with love that there is no room in our hearts for anything that is not love, that is not God.

The early Church was utterly clear that our call is to enter into the very life of God. No other objective compared with this in priority. The early Christians also knew that the way we come to this is through the human consciousness of Jesus which is to be found in the deep centre of our being. Meditation is simply the pilgrimage to the heart where we find the Spirit of Jesus worshipping the Father in love. Jesus is filled with the love for the Father that is the Father's love for him and that is

32

the Spirit. Christian meditation is simply to be open to that love which is the Spirit.

This is the plan of the universe: the purposeful call to share in the life of God in Jesus. Our tradition teaches that this call is given to everyone, not to specialists. We have only to listen to it. Anyone who takes the time to be silent will hear it in their heart. Then we respond to it simply by being wholly open to it. Cleansing our hearts and minds of everything foreign to it is the way to purity of heart. Letting go of everything that blocks it is poverty of spirit.

Meditation is the way to poverty and purity of heart. It is necessary to meditate every day and to be faithful in constancy to the mantra. That is how we leave our egoism, distraction and fear behind us. Meditation then gradually brings us to that discipline whereby we can be wholly free, wholly open to God and at one with love. Nothing could be more ordinary.

Faith's Transcendence

Meditation is the way out of our selves into God. To follow this way the most essential quality is faith. We have to leave everything behind and to become utterly poor in order to enter the presence of God and for this we need faith.

The more you invest in something the greater the faith, not less. The further you travel down a road the greater the faith and commitment. This is why faith takes us utterly beyond ourselves. Belief is a close ally of faith but they are not identical. Belief always remains somehow 'my' belief. Because of this possessiveness we can cling to our beliefs. We can impose our beliefs on others. Belief remains in the limited round of human consciousness.

Faith breaks through the circle of our self-encapsulation. We break out of the circle of what is merely human and into the divine. Faith is faith in God. It is inherently transcendent and when fully lived it calls for a generosity on our part which must be infinite and therefore for which we must reach beyond ourselves. Faith leads to sharing in the nature of God and therefore it is the way to an infinite expansion of spirit.

Meditation is sometimes called the prayer of faith because during our time of meditation we let go of everything by which we know that we are and everything that we think we are. We simply let it go. There is no need to count the cost and no advantage in trying to salvage anything from the bankruptcy.

Glory follows this great poverty. St Peter describes it as the utter freedom of spirit that sweeps us into the presence of God's timeless and spaceless glory. We are summoned to this, according to the New Testament, now, in this life. It is not just a future glory. Enlightenment with the light of Christ is a present reality, a new way of living in this world. During the time of meditation we are absorbing the knowledge of faith that we are not obliged to live merely on the material level of reality. We learned from the faith and generosity of Christ, according to St Paul, that every one of us is summoned to the new, eternal level of reality called Spirit.

This needs to be said and said again. We all need to be encouraged to tread the way faithfully day by day as we return to our morning and evening meditation. We don't need to be encouraged in the progress we are making. That would be altogether too self-conscious an approach to prayer and far too egotistical. Yet we need to take heart constantly and to be encouraged by reflecting on what God has accomplished in Jesus. Looked at from his point of view it is his glory that matters. From our perspective (as long as this is separate) it is our faith, not our progress that matters. We should, in the great poverty of the mantra, leave even our progress behind. The way of faith is also the way of humility.

> Humble yourselves then under God's mighty hand, and he will lift you up in due time. (1 Pet 5:6)

This faithful humility and humble fidelity is the way of meditation. Every time we sit down to meditate we humbly leave everything behind and make ourselves as fully available as we can to the power of God released in our hearts. We must learn to be awake, to be alert. Not, as usual, alert only to ourselves, our ideas, fears and desires, but alert to God.

Christian prayer is not only attention to God but it is coming to fullness of being in God. This is our invitation and our invitation is our destiny, given to us in Jesus. Do not be discouraged, then, and do not try to rate yourself. Measuring your progress has no significance whatever. The only significant measure is the infinite power of Christ in your heart.

Meditation is the way of being, being in God, being-in-love. All that is necessary to know is that we are on the pilgrimage and that you are continuing to be faithful. Continuing to say your mantra as best you can, day by day, with growing simplicity, deepening poverty.

Awake! be on the alert! Your enemy the devil, like a roaring lion, prowls round looking for someone to devour. Stand up to him, firm in faith, and remember that your fellow Christians are going through the same kinds of suffering while they are in the world. And the God of all grace, who called you into his eternal glory in Christ, will himself, after your brief suffering, restore, establish, and strengthen you on a firm foundation. He holds dominion for ever and ever. Amen. (1 Pet 5:8–11)

The Gift of Uniqueness

An essential part of the challenge of life facing all of us is to understand the uniqueness of our own creation. It means realising that each of us (not just my self) really has an infinite value and importance. Reflect for a moment just how radically the world, our own local society, as well as our own life, would be changed if each of us could truly appreciate our uniqueness and the wonder and dignity of the gift of our own being.

It was to awaken us to this and communicate this reality that Jesus came, taught and lived out the fullness of his uniqueness. This is the message of his love as it was proved by his death. Each of us has such importance and value that 'God sent his only Son' to offer his life for us. The crucifixion is the divine plea to each of us to understand the meaning and wonder of our creation, the dignity which love bestows.

Each of us must accept the responsibility for discovering this. The Christian experience cannot be shared second-hand. Other people's experience can be instructive and inspiring but it can never substitute for our own experience. Each person is called uniquely to open his or her heart to the supreme reality of God's love. It is the unique focusing of the love with which God loves the cosmos into a being that we call a person.

In knowing this we open our hearts to the reality of our personal destiny, far beyond the narrow confines of the ego. The astonishing core of the Christian revelation is that the destiny of each person is full union with God, 'to share in the very being of God', as St Peter puts it. The mystery is that it is a universal calling and yet each of us shares it uniquely. It is your sharing of it that is your destiny. My sharing of it is my destiny. The deep sharing between us is the knowledge of this love of God, 'though it is beyond knowledge'.

Perhaps the greatest problem afflicting our society is that so many people feel that they are not fully alive. They suffer the sense that they are not fully authentic as human beings. A major reason for this is that there are so many living their life second-hand without a real openness to the uniqueness of the gift given to them: their own life.

So many lives are lived by responding to other people's goals for us, society's goals for us, the advertising industry's goals for us. Christian revelation says that each of us is summoned to respond directly to the fullness of our own life in the mystery of God. How then are we to break out of the enclosed circle of inauthenticity and its consequent lifelessness? There is only one way and it is the basic message of the New Testament: to be fully open to the gift of eternal life.

> He who believes in the Son of God has this testimony in his own heart. . . The witness is this: that God has given us eternal life, and that this life is found in his Son. (1 Jn 5:10, 11)

The gift of life to each person is itself an invitation to development – an invitation we deny or refuse at our peril. No matter what fears or desires hinder our acceptance, there is no ultimate reason why we should not be open to the 'life found in the Son' to be encountered in the deep centre of our being. We cannot live fully, wholly, richly, as we are intended to do, without this radical openness. To be open is to accept the gift and to accept is to transcend our resistances.

More and more thinkers in our society who reflect on the large questions determining our common future are coming to realise that the basic social problems are essentially spiritual. The basic problem – it is also the basic opportunity – for each person is to know who we are, what our potential is and then to realise that potential in the love of God. Meditation meets these basic questions of life for each person. Because of our commitment to its practice, meditation means we do not have to be content living at one remove from spiritual reality, merely reading about it or listening to others talking about it. The social importance of meditation is rooted in this personal dimension of spiritual experience.

The supreme Christian insight is that God is love. The supreme Christian experience, which cannot be separated from authentic insight, is to know this love in your own heart. All this is mere words – sounding brass and tinkling cymbals – unless we take practical steps to be open to the reality to which the words point.

We meditate each day because our day needs to be fully inserted within this reality. By being wholly still we become wholly open. Open to our own wholeness, the mantra brings us to a depth and wonder of attention that eventually transcends distraction. The purpose of the word is to bring us to this point of stillness and openness which is beyond all division and disharmony. Do not therefore be discouraged if the stillness and peace do not become an immediate and constant reality. There will be glimpses of this reality. But do not linger over them or try to possess them.

When you encounter the division and disharmony within yourself continue saying the word, open and faithful to the prayer of the Spirit in your heart. The weekly meditation group is a real grace to help you to persevere and to continue deepening your journey. Indeed it is a grace that we should be seeking to be open to the supreme reality that is God, that is love. The way – it cannot be said too often – is the way of simplicity. Say your word like a child and you will realise the dimensions and wisdom of this simplicity. Do not try to unravel the mystery but allow God to unfold his mystery in your heart. God will do so within the simple union of love you have in the deep centre of your being with God. It will be a personal, unique unravelling which makes a unique contribution to the universe as a whole and to the whole design of creation.

Sit down, close your eyes and say your mantra.

I Am as I Am

Perhaps you have been meditating for long enough to realise that nothing anyone can say about meditation is ever very satisfactory. If so, you will also know that the only ultimately important thing is that we meditate, treading the path of this pilgrimage each day of our lives.

Talking about a path of this kind can even be dangerous because, in the nature of language, it is so easy to imagine that by talking about it we know about it. Yet if we talked about it from now until the end of time we would know almost nothing about it.

The mystery is that if we can only learn the humility, patience and fidelity to say our mantra we can enter fully into everything there is. This is the present-ness of the mystery of God, who is, who is now, who is always, who is all. The time-bound structures of language and the ego-bound drives of desire and imagination perpetually fail to find the entrance to this mystery. The mantra, taking us into the present moment and beyond the ego, slips through the narrow gate into the city of God.

Only silence makes ultimate sense. Doing and thinking, which can become such compulsive modes of operation, do not make me who I am. It is being that makes me. What makes us who we are is God being God. God is as God is and I am as I am, which is to say I can only be in God.

Meditation is just this way of being in God. It is being open to the basic reality which is God being God and our participating in that by being in God. Saying all this, of course, is one thing. Understanding it is another thing and understanding is severely limited in the finitude and dualities of our mental perceptions. Yet understanding is like a signpost pointing to this core experience of being who we are. Life can only satisfy us if it is lived from this core. Why should we try to be anything else if God is content to be God? God is the self-communicating creativity of love. Prayer is simply full receptivity to that creative energy at the deepest, most real centre of our being where we are nothing but what we are. Here, beyond all effort and self-projection, all guilt or shame and all the psychological operations, we explode into the realisation of being known by the One who is.

Perhaps you have been meditating for long enough to know that it is not the thoughts or feelings that are important. God as the centre of our soul is important. When we talk of finding our own centre we mean finding God. Yet language here is one-sided. Meditation is equally being found by God.

Stillness takes us into the silence beyond the lopsidedness of language. It restores us to the inner equilibrium from which we can then use language more precisely and truthfully. But we are still so that God may find us in our finding of him at the deepest level of our being.

This is why faithfulness to the daily meditation and to our mantra during those meditation times is everything. We know that we must not think about God or imagine God during these all-important times, simply because he is present. He is there, not just to be found, but to be loved. Being in love we let thoughts fall away.

> I am convinced that there is nothing in death or in life, in the realm of spirits or superhuman powers, in the world as it is or the world as it shall be, in the forces of the universe, in heights or depths – nothing in all creation that can separate us from the love of God in Christ Jesus our Lord. (Rom 8:38–39)

What need then to be discouraged by our distractions?

Dropping the Anchor

The word 'meditation' has an interesting possible connection with the Latin *sto in medio* – 'I stand in the centre'. Meditation indeed means learning to live out of the centre of your being.

It is not an esoteric practice. Everyone needs to learn that rootedness in their centre so that they can be fully themselves. It is something deeply ordinary and natural. We live in a world that makes great demands on us and is continually threatening our ability to stay rooted in the centre of our being. Stress and all its related forms of dysfunction, depression, anxiety and addiction are not rare conditions in modern living. It is perhaps difficult to think of modern life at all without them.

One of the qualities that define the monastic life is what St Benedict calls 'stability'. The Rule of St Benedict for monasteries, what he pointedly calls 'a little rule for beginners', presents stability as one of the principal means and objectives by which a person can come to live their Christianity to the full. This quality is not regarded as esoteric or privileged, any more than meditation itself.

To be stable we need to be sure of ourselves. We need to feel we are standing on firm ground and that we will not have our identity or self-respect blown away by the first storms of disappointment or conflict which we encounter. Meditation is the way to this first and basic sense of stability, rootedness in ourselves. Without it external or physical stability can degenerate into a search for security or ways of self-protection. The essential stability is the reality of our own being, and how many are in touch with that?

The first step is always to be firmly anchored in this personal reality and to enjoy the confidence it bestows, so we are able to take the next step which is to let go of ourselves.

Saying the mantra is like dropping the anchor. It falls into the depths of our being; and it is there we have to go, far below the surface, however unfamiliar this transition may at first be. We are so caught up in dealing with all that is going on on the surface that we do not give the time to stand aside from these passing concerns. Stress, anxiety, depression can all be invoked as reasons for avoiding meditation, because of a lack of time.

But time is what we have to give it, each morning and evening. Think of it not so much as a time for 'doing' meditation as simply a time for being. Try not to get uptight about meditation itself, if at all possible! It is time for being yourself. It is not necessary to justify or defend yourself or make yourself acceptable to God or your gods. Be practical about the time. Set aside a minimum of twenty minutes which you can gradually extend to twenty-five and up to the optimum of half an hour. During that time learn to say your mantra from the beginning to the end.

This is the most effective onslaught on egoism. We assume that our ideas, thoughts and fantasies are of supreme importance. We actually identify ourselves with them very often. In meditation we learn to let them all go so that we can be. Once we touch the ground of our being we make an extraordinary discovery. We are not our ideas or ego-projections. And final rootedness, real stability can only come when we are firmly anchored in God. The discovery we are heading for when we begin to meditate is that once we are anchored in ourselves we are anchored in God.

This is a supremely human moment and we do not know what it is to be fully human until we have experienced it. But we discover at the same time our immense fragility. We can so easily be tossed around by the storms of life. Few people have escaped some experience of shipwreck. Yet along with this encounter with our woundedness and vulnerability, which it takes some courage to accept, there also comes a discovery of our infinite potential.

Our destiny calls each of us to enter into the ground of our being. It is the call to be one with God. The meaning of this destiny is that we no longer need to live isolated, self-diminishing lives. We can live in a resonant harmony with others, with God. It means we are called to be in a state of continuous expansion beyond the boundaries of our own limited being. Returning to meditation each day proves just how far we can find this expansion beyond our limitations deep within us.

To enter our own spiritual reality – dropping the anchor – is to awaken to this world of limitless development. It is the root and source of all relationship and so of all community. Our very capacity for true relationship, that is for something not based on mere self-interest, indicates we have a potential for self-transcendence. Just how much potential is what we are meant to discover.

Relationship, community and authentic progress are possible because each person possesses within the energy and conscious-ness necessary to defeat isolation, selfishness and death. Through our daily meditation we become one with this divine energy and consciousness. It is the power of the Spirit to expand us into generosity, life and love, indeed into eternal, which means limitless, life.

We must only be anchored in God. To be in his presence we have first to be wholly present to ourselves. This is where we begin, learning to be present to ourselves, far beyond self-consciousness, as we learn to say the mantra.

> He who dwells in me, as I dwell in him, bears much fruit; for apart from me you can do nothing. . . If you dwell in me, and my words dwell in you, ask what you will, and you shall have it. This is my Father's glory, that you bear fruit in plenty and so be my disciples. As the Father has loved me, so I have loved you. Dwell in my love. If you heed my commands, you will dwell in my love, as I have heeded my Father's commands and dwell in his love. (Jn 15:5, 7–10)

To dwell, to abide, to remain in the love of God: these are excellent ways to describe meditation.

Truth of the Spirit

As the mission of Jesus was ending, with the gift of his life for the world, he announced to his disciples the coming of the Paraclete – the Advocate, the Comforter, the Spirit of Truth. Let us reflect on this Spirit of Truth.

All of us are called to knowledge, to know God with a fullness that propels us beyond mere conceptual knowledge into love. To know God is to love God. The only way we can come to this knowledge is through the Spirit. For St John the principal office of the Spirit is to bear testimony to Christ. The Spirit in our hearts leads us to this knowledge of Christ which becomes love and which then takes us beyond ourselves, with Christ, into God.

As followers in our time of Christ as our master we have to remember the full significance of this call to knowledge. It is the summons to truth in its absolute fullness and in all its power to liberate us from ignorance and fear. As disciples of this master we do not give a mere notional nod to Christ. We don't just tip our caps to his presence in the world, our lives and hearts. As his followers we must keep in mind and heart everything that he once said to us and everything he has done for us. Life and time indeed are given to us so that we can grasp the true and full meaning of his coming, his teaching, his love and his death and resurrection.

Coming to knowledge of Christ brings us to grasp the full meaning of our own life as well as the meaning of the lives of those we love and share life with. The greatest tragedy of a human life would be to mistake its meaning. The tragedy of Romeo was that he misread the situation at the climactic moment of the drama, thinking that Juliet was dead. So can each of us easily mistake the meaning of an event by judging

45

it by its appearance alone. So easily can we miss the mystery of life's inner meaning.

In meditation, as we go beyond appearances, we seek to open ourselves – our deep centre – to the mystery of our creation so that we can, at depth, comprehend the gift of God in Christ. We can do so only in faith which is our capacity for self-transcendence. Faith leads us into the truth that Christ is our redeemer and that we are already redeemed. As we come to this truth we are led to be totally committed to it. This is essential in all discipleship: not to be half-hearted but fully responsive in our openness to his gift of our life and of his love in our life.

In his gospel St John teaches that the person of faith must be 'of the truth' and truth is conceived of as something growing and dynamic. It is not enough to think of accepting the faith once and for all. Faith is not a static condition. The indwelling Spirit of Truth continually influences and forms us. The importance of our daily return to meditation is that it deepens our openness and responsiveness to the Spirit's vivifying and enlightening presence.

In meditation we are constantly being refreshed by the power of the Spirit as it teaches us how to commit ourselves and dedicate ourselves to the truth. This is the truth that God is, that God is one and that our meaning is to be one with him. John describes Jesus telling us that only the person who abides in the Word can fulfil this meaning and come to a genuine knowledge.

The gospel tells us that if we make the journey to our heart, and through our heart, into the truth who is Christ we come to the inner freedom that the truth brings. 'The truth will set you free.' Truth liberates us from desire and sin. It frees us from domination by the egotistical father of lies. All that is required is total commitment.

St John makes it abundantly clear that each of us is invited to allow the Word of God – the truth of God – to abide actively and potently in our hearts. It is when it does so that we go beyond falsehood and sin. One of the things Christians are so guilty of is underestimating this vocation and destiny. Each of us is destined to come to fullness of life through the full power

of the Spirit's love. Our task is simply to come into full contact
with the Spirit of Truth by turning aside from all illusion, and
the desire that breeds illusion; to be one with him, in him.

While I am still in the world I speak these words, so that
[those who listen to me] may have my joy within them in full
measure. I have delivered thy word to them. . . I pray thee,
not to take them out of the world, but to keep them from
the evil one. . . Consecrate them by the truth; thy word is
truth. As thou hast sent me into the world, I have sent them
into the world, and for their sake I now consecrate myself,
that they too may be consecrated by the truth. (Jn 17:13–19)

This is simply what meditation is about: being consecrated by
the truth that dwells in our hearts in power.

Belief and Faith

I recently took part in a huge Catholic conference at the Anaheim Conference Center in southern California. It was an extraordinary experience in many ways. There were about 18,000 people participating; all, it seemed to me, seriously interested in deepening the Christian dimension in their lives.

They were responding to it, I suppose, in a typically American Catholic way. Each evening I would get little notes under my door saying 'the Sacred Heart invites you to drinks in Room 1222', or 'the Little Flower will have a happy hour tomorrow evening'. Yet I was deeply moved by the last group I spoke to which consisted of about 8000 people. We all meditated together, and their openness to become so silent was really inspiring.

My time there made me feel that the great problem we face today is one of commitment. For the Christian this often seems to be a question of committing oneself to certain beliefs or the behaviour based on those beliefs. Much of our religious response is indeed based primarily upon our beliefs. But I have come to feel that what we 'believe' is not really that important. Belief is like the tip of an iceberg. What matters is faith. For the Christian this means our deep commitment to Christ to the point of self-transcendence, at the very bedrock of our being.

Beliefs have to be couched in language. And language is necessary to keep the world going, of course – especially large conferences. I doubt whether 18,000 people would come a long way just to be silent together!

When I was studying Eucharistic theology the key word was 'transubstantiation'. Since then all sorts of words, including 'transfinalisation', have been proposed by theologians as more suitable for portraying what it means. Words define beliefs.

Words change. And so beliefs change. Beliefs are entirely secondary to faith which does not change. This is our faith – meaning our transcendental commitment – to Jesus Christ. The task of life is to make contact with this faith, to reach what is essential by going beyond everything that is peripheral. The clear message of the New Testament is that Jesus Christ is essential and that what he communicates to us is his essence – his own being.

However, language like this – being, essence and so on – can quickly lead to confusion. Meditation is of such supreme importance because it does not rest content with the mere formulations and propositions of language. It goes beyond the sign-realm of language to the reality, the rock-bed of meaning who is Christ.

> So come to him, our living Stone – the stone rejected by men but choice and precious in the sight of God. Come, and let yourselves be built, as living stones, into a spiritual temple; become a holy priesthood, to offer spiritual sacrifices to God through Jesus Christ. (1 Pet 2:4–5)

These words of St Peter characterise the perennial call to faith for the Christian. We have ourselves to understand, and we have to communicate to our contemporaries, that this journey of faith is a journey into value. We discover that each of us, you reading this and me writing it, is precious in the sight of God. This journey is possible for us even as ordinary persons of average talents and abilities.

We are all called to tread this inner pilgrimage. Rooting our life in the spiritual reality is part of the plan of salvation – the meaning of the universe – revealed and actually completed in Jesus. Our task is simply to get on to the wavelength of this achievement. We do not have to accomplish it ourselves – to try to would be the highest hubris.

Putting ourselves into harmony with him is the work of the mantra. The mantra is a tuning device, a harmonic to help us to resonate with Jesus. By its means we are enabled, as St Peter puts it, to let ourselves be built as living stones into a spiritual temple. By our commitment to meditating daily we take this option. By setting aside those two half-hours we move

49

from the realm of materialistic expectations and conditions in order to enter the supreme reality of God revealed in Jesus. Reality does not exist outside of us, or even inside of us. It is in the heart where all dualities are resolved and there is simply God, perfect wholeness.

During the conference in California I was most struck by the desperate need the world has for people who are rooted and grounded in faith. This means, for us, to be rooted in Christ as people who know the spiritual reality that is beyond knowledge and yet to which they are summoned as their personal destiny. People who realise the grandeur of that reality and calling are utterly humble and yet confident of the goodness and compassion of God. People who are confident without humility can be dangerous. Such religious confidence can be the most dangerous of all. But the world desperately needs people whose confidence is rooted in the humility of love.

Such people who undertake the pilgrimage into the true security of love, become grace for their world – for their friends and family, which is our first world. They are grace for the world at large as well, because this pilgrimage is a journey into sanity. Health and wholeness bestow the real, not the mock or artificial, value which has so deluded us today.

The ultimate value is God's love for each of us as well as for all creation. These two are really one, as God, being one, does not divide his love. He loves all or nothing, and does so equally because he loves absolutely. Human value – and God's love for us gives us this value – is personal. Faith, which is the transcendent point of encountering this love, must also be utterly personal. It must be your own faith, not somebody else's belief you have inherited or absorbed. You will encounter this faith in your own heart and in doing so meet God in the heart of Jesus.

The congress reminded me again of the importance for Christians of regaining a real sense of the magnificence of our calling.

You are a chosen race, a royal priesthood, a dedicated nation, and a people claimed by God for his own, to proclaim the triumphs of him who has called you out of darkness into his marvellous light. You are now the people of God, who once were not his people; outside his mercy once, you have now received his mercy. (1 Pet 2:9–10)

Every time we meditate, alone or in a group, we respond to this call from darkness into his marvellous light.

All You have to Do is Begin

To learn to meditate you have to learn to be silent and not to be afraid of silence. A great difficulty presents itself to many modern people who are beginning to meditate simply because they are so unused to silence. Even at our meditation groups, we usually play some music as people assemble rather than prepare in complete silence, because many would feel very uncomfortable walking into a room of silent strangers. Travelling to California recently I witnessed this conversation, or something like it, between two men sitting near me: one said 'Going somewhere?', to which the other rather surprisingly replied 'No'. There was an embarrassed pause after which the first person said hopefully, 'I've just been there. Now I'm going back'.

Many of us spend a great deal of time in such inane conversation because we are so frightened and feel so socially awkward of silent spaces in our meeting together. We fear silence when we are alone as well and so we often live with a constant background of radio chat shows or muzak.

In meditation we cross the threshold from background noise into silence. This is vital for us because silence is necessary if the human spirit is to thrive and to be creative. Silence releases a creative response to life, to our environment and friends because it gives our spirit room to breathe, room to be. In silence we do not have to justify ourselves, apologise or impress anyone. Just be.

It is a most marvellous experience of liberty. In silence you are not playing a role or fulfilling any expectations. You are just there, realising your being, open to reality. Then, in the Christian vision, you are overwhelmed by the discovery that the reality in which we have our being is love. In silence we know that our spirit is expanding into love.

To learn to be silent is to begin a journey. All you have to do is to begin. To take the first step into the silence is to begin the journey of your life, the journey into life. You are learning two things: firstly, to sit still, not because you are afraid to move or are imposing a burden on yourself, but because in stillness you seek a unity of body, mind and spirit; secondly, to recite your mantra in response to the deepening silence that arises in stillness.

As you begin to say your mantra you become aware that you are on the threshold of silence. This is a critical moment for most people, as they leave the familiar world of sounds, ideas, thoughts, words and images. You do not know what is in store for you as you cross into the silence. This is why it is so important to learn to meditate in a tradition and in a group that receives, passes on and embodies that tradition. It is for us a tradition that says 'fear not'. Jesus is the heart of a tradition that sees the purpose of meditation as being in the presence of love, the love that casts out all fear.

The threshold of silence is still a critical moment because if you go back to your thoughts and images, even perhaps to your familiar prayers, you have turned away from the door to silence which leads into the pure prayer of love. Learning to return humbly to your mantra is the first step into this wonderful experience of silence as the presence of love.

I could use all the words in our vocabulary to tell you about the eternal silence of God that dwells within our innermost being, the silence of pure creation. I could say how important that silence is because in it you hear your own name spoken clearly and unmistakably for the first time. You come to know who you are. Yet all these words would fail to convey the experience itself – an experience of unself-conscious liberty in the creating presence of God.

To learn to be silent is to say your mantra and to keep saying it. So do not fear to leave your thoughts behind. Do not go back to your ideas or imaginations. Leave them to one side and say your word. We are not alone in doing this.

And from time to time he would withdraw to lonely places for prayer. . . During this time he went out one day into the hills to pray, and spent the night in prayer to God. (Lk 5:16; 6:12)

When we meditate in this tradition we enter into this same silence and it makes us one with Jesus in God.

Integrity

We recommend people who come to our introductory meditation groups to come for about ten weeks. Then, if and when they feel like it, they can transfer to a weekly ongoing group. People sometimes ask me what is the difference between the groups and often like to think of the second group as the 'group for proficients'. But I think the difference is really that in the first group people are hearing of the simplicity and stillness of meditation, and in the second group they are being reminded of the need to become more silent and more still.

It often seems as if we rush through life at such high speed while in our heart there is the essential interior flame of being. Our rushing often brings it to the point of extinction. But when we sit down to meditate, in stillness and simplicity, the flame begins to burn brightly and steadily. As we abandon thinking in terms of success and self-importance, the light of the flame helps us to understand ourselves and others in terms of light, warmth and love.

The mantra leads us to this point of stillness where the flame of being can burn bright. It teaches us what we know, but frequently forget, that we cannot live a full life unless it is grounded on some underlying purpose. Life has an ultimate significance and value that is only really discovered in the still steadiness of being which is our essential rootedness in God.

It is terribly easy to let life become mere routine. Roles can easily take the place of being. We fall into playing the routine roles of student, mother, husband, manager, monk or whatever that we find we are wearing. Jesus came to tell us that life is not about playing roles or being a functionary in some system. It is about meaning and purpose felt in the depth of our stillest being. Our value arises from who we are in ourselves, not what we do in a role-image of ourselves.

The ultimate meaning of God does not arise from what society says we are – that would be to 'prefer human approval to the approval of God', as Jesus put it. When St Thomas More was imprisoned in the Tower of London for preferring his conscience to the approval of the king, his public role was destroyed and he became a common criminal. Yet his integrity was not destroyed. He knew who he was not only in the eyes of the world, or even his own eyes, but in the eyes of God. He enjoyed a profound confidence arising from the true depth of self-knowledge which let him know who he was eternally – created by God, redeemed by Jesus and a temple of the Holy Spirit.

Each of us similarly, but in terms of our unique destiny, must discover the fundamental truth about ourselves. Rooted in God, we must be open to the love that redeems us from illusion and shallowness. We must live out of that personal infinite holiness which we have as a temple of the Holy Spirit. Discovering that the same Spirit which created the universe dwells in our hearts, and in silence is loving to all, is the purpose of every life.

We must be as radical, in our own way, as Thomas More in order to fulfil this purpose. Everyone around him tried to dissuade him from his integrity. And we live in a society that does not recognise the crucial value of spiritual practice because it has forgotten the spiritual reality.

Meditation is a practice that enables us each day to root our lives in the spiritual reality of God. It is a positive way, even though our current materialistic and outer-directed values may dismiss it as a waste of time or as unproductive introversion. Yet in meditation we do not reject the world or construct any false opposition to it. We wish to live fully in the world but we know we can only arrive at that fullness and wholeheartedness if we are truly rooted in God.

Learning to meditate is quite a demand. It means devoting time generously to what is the most important fact in life, that God is and that the Spirit of God dwells in our hearts. In meditating we accept that fact and adopt a wholly positive attitude to it. It is not only death we often suppress and deny, it is also God and therefore life. Each day needs to be begun out of the acceptance of God's power in our life. Each day needs to be brought to a conclusion by returning our scattered minds to the mystery of his presence and love.

Integrity means wholeness. Meditation is a way that brings every part of our day, all our experience and all the dimensions of our being, into harmony. It is the way beyond the personal dividedness and anxiety from which we suffer as a result of our denial of God and our separation from the Spirit. Meditation proves itself, through faithful practice, as a way to deep peace and joy. It takes us across the bridge of sadness that arises from the feeling of separation. The ego arises in separateness and when the ego is transcended we realise our unity with God.

> The Son of God, Christ Jesus, proclaimed among you by us . . . was never a blend of Yes and No. With him it was, and is, Yes. He is the Yes pronounced upon God's promises, every one of them. That is why, when we give glory to God, it is through Jesus Christ that we say 'Amen'. And if you and we belong to Christ, guaranteed as his and anointed, it is all God's doing; it is God also who has set his seal upon us, and as a pledge of what is to come has given us the Spirit to dwell in our hearts. (2 Cor 1:19–22)

With Jesus, St Paul tells us, it was only Yes. With us, too, there must be an affirmative attitude to life and to the essential fact of life which is the Spirit dwelling in our hearts. In meditation our purpose is to become wholly at one with that presence, wholly present to the presence.

Purity of Heart

The greatest need of our time is for men and women who are confident in the gift of their own life. As Christians, they would be people whose lives are lived out of that power released into the world through the life, death and resurrection of Jesus.

Meditation is our commitment to the reality of that power of Jesus set free in the world and flowing in our hearts. Once we have plunged into this sea of the Spirit the gift to be tasted is liberty. We are made free by the power of that life, death and resurrection. We often think of freedom merely as the freedom to do what we want to do. But even the most rudimentary experience of making contact with the power of Jesus in meditation shows us that freedom is not essentially the power to do but the liberty to be who we are: the redeemed, the loved of Christ.

To be who we are, we must be in relationship. We often painfully discover that we cannot be ourselves in isolation. The fundamental relationship of life is our relationship with God, and meditation is our commitment to that. Prayer could be described as the selfless attention we bring to this relationship in which all relationships find their source. So we do not think about ourselves in meditation. We attend to God. Even to think of God would lead us to thinking of God in terms of ourselves.

Jesus tells us that 'only God is good': that is, God is all-goodness quite transcending human ideas of the good. The wonder of prayer is that, in selfless attention, we enter God's all-goodness and become good ourselves; not through any kind of platonic striving but simply because we enter the radiance of the orbit of his goodness. This is the essential basis of all morality, not that we try to imitate God but that we participate in the goodness of God.

The ancient Fathers called this 'purity of heart'. It is enjoyed when our heart is cleansed of all desire, including the desire for God. We should not want to possess God or even to possess wisdom or happiness. Desire itself prevents us from enjoying any of these. We should rather, simply and in quiet stillness, be who we are and be content to be good because we are in God.

We all come from a state we once enjoyed of simplicity, innocence and the joy of sheer goodness. This is the basis of a truly religious response to life. You can see this in the serious eyes of a child who is beginning to discover the wonder in the mystery of life, in religion, in God. Meditation is so important to all of us because, by the simplifying power of its action, it brings us again to this serious approach to religious experience.

By serious, I mean that in meditation we are not trying to manipulate God for our own purposes. We are not condescending to involve him in our lives. We are rather discovering the wonder of his involvement in our life. We do so by saying the mantra, coming to stillness and silence, going beyond desire and coming to purity of heart. We are then simply open – but this requires everything we are – to reality in its purest and most intimate self-revelation.

We are open to God's presence, within us and around us, as the power that sustains us by love. We live in the presence of the One who purifies us by his love and who renews us with boundless energy from an infinite source of love. When this love encounters our woundedness, our desires and illusions, our egotism, we call it forgiveness.

Never forget the purity of heart involved in saying the mantra. Faithfulness to the mantra from the beginning to the end of every meditation brings us to this simplicity and innocence because it enables us to leave self behind. The confidence to proclaim Christ, the discretion needed to see how we should do this today, and the courage to witness to Christ from our own experience of him, arises from our fidelity to meditation each day and to the mantra.

There is nothing less shining in our hearts than the glory of

Christ. That glory is not triumphalist but it does triumph over hearts hardened by the wounds of life. Poverty, purity, simplicity are strange weapons to minds trained on images and values of violence. But our survival, spiritually and even physically, depends upon our recovering an awareness of the redeeming power of these qualities of humanity. This is the way of the mantra.

It is not ourselves that we proclaim; we proclaim Christ Jesus as Lord, and ourselves as your servants, for Jesus' sake. For the same God who said, 'Out of darkness let light shine', has caused his light to shine within us, to give the light of revelation – the revelation of the glory of God in the face of Jesus Christ. (2 Cor 4:5–6)

How to Meditate

Sit down. Sit still and upright. Close your eyes lightly. Sit relaxed but alert. Silently, interiorly begin to say a single word. We recommend the prayer-phrase "maranatha." Recite it as four syllables of equal length. Listen to it as you say it, gently but continuously. Do not think or imagine anything – spiritual or otherwise. If thoughts and images come, these are distractions at the time of meditation, so keep returning to simply saying the word. Meditate each morning and evening for between twenty and thirty minutes.

The World Community for Christian Meditation

Meditation creates community. Since the first Christian Meditation Centre was started by John Main in 1975, a steadily growing community of Christian meditators has spread around the world. Individual meditators frequently begin to meet in small weekly groups and the network of these groups provides wider support and encouragement for those who wish to sustain their daily practice of morning and evening meditation.

The groups meet in homes, parishes schools, prisons, business, religious communities and government departments. Beginning with a short teaching on meditation, often drawn from the Community's collection of taped talks by John Main, the group then meditates together in silence for half an hour. After the talk, there is time for discussion. The groups are by nature ecumenical and practice an open-door hospitality, welcoming anyone who comes sincerely seeking silence.

A growing number of Christian Meditation Centres, some residential, others located in meditators' homes, also serve to communicate the way of silence taught in this tradition. The Centres help co-ordinate the local weekly groups and organize regular retreats, seminars and other meditation events.

The International Centre in London co-ordinates this world-wide community of meditators. A quarterly newsletter, giving spiritual teaching and reflection, is sent out from London and distributed from a number of national centers, together with local and international news of retreats and other events being held in the world-wide community. An annual John Main Seminar is held in Europe and North America on alternate years.

This Centre is funded entirely by donations and especially through a Friends of the International Centre programme.

The World Community for Christian Meditation
International Centre
23 Kensington Square
London W8 5HN
United Kingdom
Tel: 44 171 937 4679 Fax: 44 171 937 6790
E-mail: wccm@compuserve.com

Visit The World Community for Christian Meditation Web site for information, weekly mediation group reading and discussion at: **www.wccm.org**

John Main

John Main was born in London in 1926 into an Irish family. He studied law, learned Chinese and then served in the British Foreign Service in Malaysia. There he was introduced to meditation by an Indian monk. At that time silent, non-conceptual prayer was a rare and unfamiliar practice for most Christians. After his service in the east, John Main returned to Europe where he continued his meditation practice as the foundation of his Christian life. He became a professor of international law at Trinity College, Dublin.

John Main became a Benedictine monk in 1958 in London. In 1969 he rediscovered a Christian tradition of meditation, of "pure prayer" as it was called, taught by the Desert Fathers, the first Christian monks, to St. Benedict and the Western church.

Having returned to his practice of meditation, John Main then dedicated the rest of his life to teaching this lost tradition of Christian prayer to lay people of all ages and walks of life. He believed it was important for the world to restore a spiritual practice of depth to people's ordinary lives. He recommended two periods of meditation, each morning and evening, which could also be integrated with other forms of prayer.

John Main died in 1982. His work and vision is continued by a growing world-wide network of Christian meditation groups and centers.

Medio Media Ltd.

Medio Media Ltd. is the publishing arm of the World Community for Christian Meditation. It is committed to the dissemination of the teaching of meditation in the Christian tradition and, in particular, to the work of John Main. It is further committed to the growing dialogue among meditators and seekers from all traditions based on the experience of silence shared by all religions.

A catalog of Medio Media's publications—books, audio sets and videos—is available from:

Medio Media Ltd

23 Kensington Square
London W8 5HN
United Kingdom
Tel: 44 171 937 4679 Fax: 44 171 937 6790
E-mail: wccm@compuserve.com

Christian Mediation Centres

International Centre: 23 Kensington Square / London W8 5HN / United Kingdom.
Tel: 44 171 937 4679 Fax: 44 171 937 6790
E-mail: wccm@compuserve.com

Australia: Australian Christian Meditation Community / PO Box 66390 / St. Kilda Rd. Central / Victoria 3004.
Tel/Fax: 61 7 3300 or 61 3 9435 8943
E-mail: acmchall@Bigpond.com

Belgium: Christelijk Meditatie Centrum / Beiaardlaan 1 / 1850 Grimbergen.
Tel/Fax: 32 2 269 5071

Brazil: Christa Meditacao Communidade / C.P. 33266 / CEP 22442-970 / Rio de Janeiro / RJ.
Tel: 55 21 512 3806 Fax: 55 21 294 7995
E-mail: smorais@ibm.net

Canada: Christian Meditation Community / PO Box 552 / Station NDG / Montreal / Quebec H4A 3P9.
Tel: 1 514 766 0475 Fax: 1 514 937 8178
E-mail: mark.schofield@sympatico.ca

Centre de Méditation Chrétienne / Cap Vie / 367 boul. Ste Rose / Laval / QC H71 1N3.
Tel/Fax: 1 514 625 0133

Germany: Christliche Meditationszentrum / c/o Gunter Meng / C4, 16 / D-68159 Mannheim.
Tel: 49 171 268 6245 Fax: 49 40 3603 095 720
E-mail: GueMeng@aol.com

India: Christian Meditation Centre / 1/1429 Bilathikulam Road / Calicut / 673006 Kerala.
Tel: 91 33 495 50395

Ireland: Christian Meditation Centre / 4 Eblana Ave. / Dun Laoghaire / Co. Dublin.
Tel: 353 1 280 1505 Fax: 353 1 280 8720

Italy: Centro di Meditazione Christiana / Abbazia di San Miniato al Monte / Via Delle Porte Sante 34 / 50125 Firenze.
Tel/Fax: 39 55 247 6302

Malaysia: Christian Meditation Centre / 7 Jalan Pekaka Dua / SG. Dua / Gelogor / Pulau Pinang 11700 / Malaysia.
Tel: 60 4 657 7414
E-mail: saymooi@tm.net.my

New Zealand: Christian Meditation Centre / PO Box 35531 / Auckland 1310.

Philippines: Christian Meditation Centre / 11 Osmeña St. / South Admiral Village / Bgy Merville / Pque. / MM 1760
Tel: 63 2 824 9595 Fax: 63 2 823 3742

Singapore: Christian Meditation Centre / 9 Mayfield Avenue / Singapore 438 023.
Tel: 65 348 6790 Fax: 65 348 7302

Thailand: Christian Meditation Centre / 51/1 Sedsiri Road / Bangkok 10400.
Tel: 66 2 271 3295 Fax: 66 2 271 2632
E-mail: sketudat@mozart.inet.co.th

United Kingdom: Christian Meditation Centre / The Hermitage / Monastery of Christ the King / 29 Bramley Road / Cockfosters / London N14 4HE.
Tel/Fax: 44 181 441 0680
E-mail: crncuk@compuserve.com

United States: Christian Meditation Centre / 1080 West Irving Park Rd. / /Roselle, IL 60172.
Tel/Fax: 1 630 351 2613

John Main Institute / 7315 Brookville Rd. / Chevy Chase, MD 20815.
Tel: 1 301 652 8635
E-mail: wmcoerp@erols.com

Christian Meditation Centre / 1619 Wright St. / Wall, NJ 07719.
Tel: 1 732 681 6238 Fax: 1 732 280 5999
E-mail: gjryan@aol.com

The Cornerstone Centre / 1215 East Missouri Ave. / Suite A 100 / Phoenix, AZ 85014-2914.
Tel: 1 602 279 3454 Fax: 1 602 957 3467
E-mail: ecrmjr@worldnet.att.net